The Earliest Farmers and the First Cities

Charles Higham

Published in cooperation with Cambridge University Press
Lerner Publications Company, Minneapolis

Editors' Note: In preparing this edition of *The Cambridge Topic Books* for publication, the editors have made only a few minor changes in the original material. In some isolated cases, British spelling and usage were altered in order to avoid possible confusion for our readers. Whenever necessary, information was added to clarify references to people, places, and events in British history. An index was also provided in each volume.

LIBRARY OF CONGRESS CATALOGING IN PUBLICATION DATA

Higham, Charles.
The earliest farmers and the first cities.

(A Cambridge Topic Book)
Includes index.
SUMMARY: Discusses information archaeologists have gathered about early farmers in central Turkey and on the Tigris-Euphrates plain.

1. Near East—Civilization—Juvenile literature. 2. Agriculture—Origin—Juvenile literature. [1. Near East—Civilization. 2. Agriculture—History. 3. Near East—Antiquities] I. Title.

DS57.H54 1977   935'.01   76-22425
ISBN 0-8225-1203-3

This edition first published 1977 by Lerner Publications Company by permission of Cambridge University Press.

Original edition copyright © 1974 by Cambridge University Press as part of *The Cambridge Introduction to the History of Mankind: Topic Book*.

International Standard Book Number: 0-8225-1203-3
Library of Congress Catalog Card Number: 76-22425

Manufactured in the United States of America

This edition is available exclusively from:
Lerner Publications Company, 241 First Avenue North, Minneapolis, Minnesota 55401

2 3 4 5 6 7 8 9 10 86 85

Contents

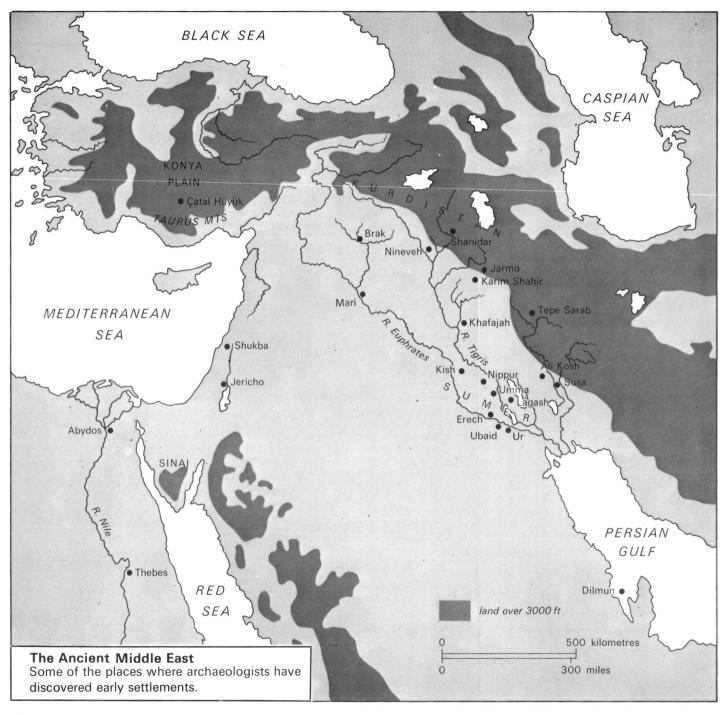

BLACK SEA

CASPIAN SEA

KONYA PLAIN

● Çatal Hüyük

TAURUS MTS

K U R D I S T A N

● Brak

● Shanidar

Nineveh ●

● Jarmo

● Karim Shahir

MEDITERRANEAN SEA

Mari ●

● Tepe Sarab

● Khafajah

R. Euphrates

R. Tigris

● Shukba

● Ali Kosh

Kish ●

● Nippur

● Susa

● Jericho

S ●Umma

U

Lagash

Abydos ●

M

Erech ●

E

R. Nile

Ubaid ●

R

● Ur

SINAI

PERSIAN GULF

● Thebes

RED SEA

Dilmun ●

land over 3000 ft

0   500 kilometres

0   300 miles

The Ancient Middle East
Some of the places where archaeologists have
discovered early settlements.

1. The first farmers

Think how important crops like wheat, corn and rice, and farm animals such as pigs, cattle and sheep are today. If they were not grown and sold by farmers, food would be very scarce. These plants and animals once lived only in the wild. For many years, archaeologists have been trying to discover where farming began, and how long ago the first farmers lived. They have discovered that farming and animal rearing began at different times in different places. The earliest rice farmers lived in Thailand over 6000 years ago. Corn was domesticated in Central America about 8000 years ago. Many archaeologists have also worked in the Middle East, where they have found evidence for the early domestication of wheat, barley, sheep and goats. More is known about the first farmers and city dwellers there than about those in America or Thailand.

How the archaeologist studies the past

How can we possibly find out where and when farming and city life began, or even if it began quite independently in more than one place at different times? In many ways the archaeologist who tries to answer these questions is like a detective. He looks for places where people once lived or buried their dead, and then, with the same skill and care as a surgeon, he cuts into the ancient village or grave. Gradually he removes the earth that has built up over the centuries, not with a pick or a shovel, but with trowel and brush. He records the exact position of everything he finds, until piece by piece he is able to build up a picture of what life was like for those long-dead people.

He finds not only the ruins, but also the rubbish of villages

Two archaeologists excavating an ancient grave. The man is uncovering two pots which contained food for the dead. In the background a gravestone and fragments of pottery and human bones are beginning to appear.

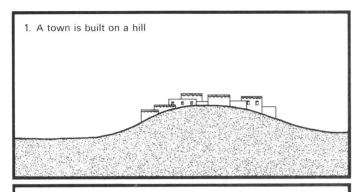

1. A town is built on a hill

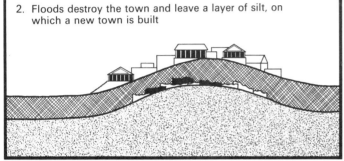

2. Floods destroy the town and leave a layer of silt, on which a new town is built

3. The second town is burned down

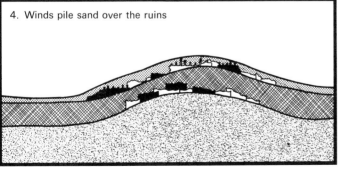

4. Winds pile sand over the ruins

deserted thousands of years ago. A line of broken bricks may tell him where people once lived, and charred animal bones may provide evidence for what the people ate. He can discover much about the people themselves from their burials. Were they tall or short? How old were they when they died? Do thin twisted bones suggest that they suffered from a meagre diet? Were any killed violently? There are pictures and stories in this book which depict life amongst the earliest farmers and in the first cities. The stories and pictures are built up from clues worked out by archaeologists.

One of the archaeologist's most important problems is to discover what type of settlement he is excavating. Sometimes, it will be a hunters' camp; at other times it could be anything from a farming village to a city. The difference between a hunters' camp and a city is obvious, but the stages in between are not always so easy to recognize.

One main difference between a farming village and a town or city is that townspeople are employed in different occupations, and are divided into different social classes. This way of living is often called 'civilization'. It is very different from the life of families and tribes of hunters and farmers.

Since large towns grew from humble farming villages, some of the settlements found by the archaeologist may be neither villages nor towns, but have some features of each. The inhabitants of these intermediate types of settlement may be described as civilized by some archaeologists, but not by others. There is no hard and fast rule for using the term 'civilization'.

Sometimes archaeologists are able to unravel the history of a particular village or town because new houses were built on top of the ruins of the old. This process, repeated time and again over the years, led to a gradual build-up in the height of the village until the last one stood on a fairly high mound. At other times the archaeologist may excavate a site where only a few stone knives and animal bones remain. In this case he will be dealing with a hunters' camp which may only have been occupied for a few hours.

Successive stages in the build-up of a prehistoric settlement mound. Archaeologists often find the remains of ancient towns one on top of another.

Expert help

On finishing a season's excavations, the archaeologist turns to other experts for assistance in studying his finds. By means of 'radiocarbon dating' (a technique which measures changes which occur once a living thing dies), physicists can tell him how long ago things like timbers from buildings, charred wood found in campfires, or shell fish collected for food, were living. This, of course, allows the archaeologist to estimate when the settlement he has been excavating was lived in.

Botanists can tell whether the village was set on a grassy plain or was hemmed in by forest by identifying the tiny pollen grains which were blown into the ancient rubbish dumps by the wind. All types of plant have distinct types of pollen grain, and these are almost indestructible. By 'pollen analysis'— that is, identifying the grains belonging to different types of plant— the botanist can tell which trees and shrubs and grasses surrounded the ancient settlements.

Careful study of the materials of which tools, weapons or ornaments were made may suggest where the original stone or metal came from. Sometimes, stone was quarried many miles from a particular village and may have been brought there by merchants. Obsidian, for example, was quarried in Turkey and traded over very wide areas. This sharp, volcanic glass was valued because it can be chipped to a very sharp edge. The tools themselves also tell the archaeologist much : axes suggest woodworking, while fish hooks point to fishing.

Scientists often discover new methods of bringing the past to life. The shape and size of animals' bones show whether cattle, sheep, goats and swine were wild, or whether they were domesticated. The analysis of charred ears of wheat or barley can tell the expert whether they were gathered wild, or were specially planted, tended and harvested in the grain fields of long ago.

The detective cannot always solve his cases, nor can the archaeologist always answer the questions he would like to. Broken bricks tell him nothing of the language people once spoke, nor do fragments of pottery usually tell what the pots contain. But scientists can now solve many riddles of the past, and allow us to reconstruct the distant beginnings of both farming and city life.

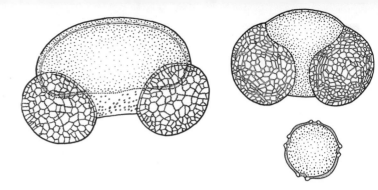

Prehistoric pollen grains of fir, spruce and hornbeam. The fir is the largest, hornbeam the smallest. They are enlarged more than 100 times.

Prehistoric wheat grains, more than 5000 years old, found by archaeologists in Greece. Below is the imprint left by a wheat grain on a fragment of a pot, together with a caste made from it.

2. From hunting to farming in the Middle East

Hunting and gathering food

Although everyone must have food and shelter, there are many different ways of obtaining them. Some people may hunt wild animals, or collect berries and plants, while others grow their food in fields, and keep domestic animals. Nowadays, many buy what they need with the money they have earned.

There was a time when all men lived by hunting and gathering their food. From the frozen wastes of Siberia, where ingenious methods were devised for trapping the fleet-footed reindeer, to the steamy forests of the Congo, where monkeys and wild pigs were killed with poisoned arrows, hunters every-where had the same problem; how to find enough food to feed their families throughout the year.

Today, there are very few hunters left. The white man brought cattle rearing to the plains of America, driving out the native 'Indian' from his hunting grounds as he went. Bantu farmers spread through Africa, sweeping the Bushman hunters in front of them. In the Polynesian islands of the Pacific, people have been farmers for over 3,000 years, growing taro and yam and breeding domestic pigs.

One of the most difficult tasks for the archaeologist is to find out when and where hunters first discovered how to domesticate animals and plants. His search must begin in those

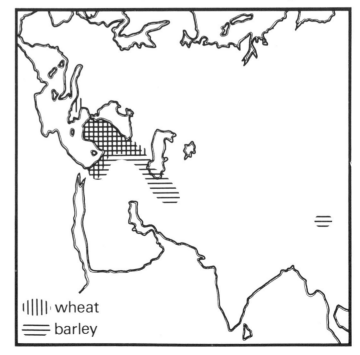

ılllll goat
≡ sheep

ılllll wheat
≡ barley

areas of the world where wheat and barley and certain farm animals once lived completely wild. (These areas are shown in the maps on page 8.)

In 1928, Professor Dorothy Garrod took a team of archaeologists to excavate the cave of Shukba, which is situated in the Judaean Hills. What they found is the first chapter in a remarkable story. After removing the topsoil at the front of the cave, they came across the burials and tools of a people who lived there 13,000 years ago. The presence of stone arrowheads and the bones of wild animals means that the people in question were hunters, who went out from the cave after the huge wild bulls, the deer and the mountain goats which lived nearby. Imagine the lives those hunters led. Sometimes they came back from the hunt flushed with success. For the next few days, there would be more than enough food for everyone. It is well known that hunters and gatherers, in order to survive, must have a detailed knowledge of the habits of the animals they hunt, and of the seasons and places where plants ripen. Therefore, it is often found that bands of hunter-gatherers move with changing seasons to places where food is normally plentiful. The Shukba hunters, like many of those who continue to hunt and forage for their food to this day, probably moved their homes several times in a year.

Evenings after a successful day's hunting were spent making new arrowheads and spears. The women, who had already spent the day under the hot sun laboriously collecting the seeds of wild grasses, were also kept busy. Some stitched decorative shells on to little leather caps, while others prepared animal skins for making clothes. These too were decorated with shells, for the Shukba hunters delighted in lively ornaments. Some of the dead were buried with their own jewellery, which included necklaces and pendants made from bone and shell.

As a result of Professor Garrod's excavations, we know that 13,000 years ago the hills and valleys near the River Jordan were populated by small bands of hunters and gatherers.

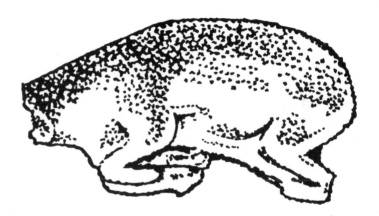

A little carving of a deer made from limestone by one of the Shukba hunters.

A necklace of carved bone from Shukba.

Farming: the first clues emerge

In 1948, a large archaeological expedition from America began to explore ancient villages which had been found on the hilly uplands bordering the Tigris-Euphrates valley. Its purpose was to find evidence for the very beginning of farming. Zoologists went to study the wild animals which live there today, and botanists went to obtain samples of pollen.

Like Professor Garrod, they found the area had once been occupied by hunters. From places like Karim Shahir and Shanidar, the early hunters had combed the area for food, shooting deer and gazelle, tracking down turtles and collecting huge quantities of shellfish.

After the excavations were over, all the finds were packed in wooden crates and shipped from the hot uplands of Iraqi Kurdistan, across the Atlantic Ocean, to America. Animal bones, thousands of fragments of flint, stone beads, bracelets and pendants were cleaned, labelled and carefully examined.

It was the zoologists who discovered the first clue. There were many more sheep bones at Shanidar than at the other sites. Why was this? Could it be that the hunters went to that area because of its abundance of wild sheep? Now came a second clue. Many of the bones were from very young lambs. It was almost as if lambs had been born at the settlement of Shanidar. If this was the case, then could it be possible that the Shanidar hunters deliberately kept sheep near their homes, in the world's first domestic flock?

The scientists then turned their attention to the other finds from Shanidar and Karim Shahir. They recognized a number of millstones. Perhaps they were used for grinding wheat into flour? They then identified small stone hoes, and some flint knives with a brilliant polish along their cutting edges. This polish may well have been caused by the continual cutting of tough grain stalks.

All these scraps of evidence suggested that the hunters of Karim Shahir and Shanidar had discovered the secret of farming. Now the archaeologists turned to the physicists to find out how long ago the sites were occupied. The answer came back: about 11,800 years ago. The expedition could now be pronounced a success; it had located and dated the homes of the earliest farmers yet known in the Middle East.

Excavations did not stop with these discoveries. Further work at sites like Ali Kosh, Jarmo, Tepe Sarab and Jericho has allowed archaeologists to reconstruct many details of the way of life of those early farmers.

For at least 30,000 years, the ancestors of the early farmers had moved their camps seasonally from one area to another, to hunt wild animals and to collect roots, seeds and nuts when they were ripe. These same bands of hunters and gatherers also traded raw materials, such as obsidian, and bitumen, which was used for fixing spears. They could have traded bags of edible seeds for obsidian and dried meat for bitumen.

No one can be certain how plants were first domesticated. It is thought that perhaps seeds of wild wheat and barley were traded over considerable distances. Some may have been lost on the way, and so sprouted in places where they did not grow naturally. Perhaps some hunters realized what had happened, and saw that it would be possible to plant wild seeds deliberately for a later harvest. So the discovery of agriculture was made.

Equally, no one is sure how sheep or goats were first domesticated. Perhaps the mother of a new-born lamb was killed, and the hunter took the tiny orphan back to camp to show his children. The same lamb may have grown up accustomed to

The mound in the centre of the photograph is the site of Karim Shahir.

Some blades made of chipped flint which were used to cut wheat. (Actual size.)

above: A stone mortar and part of a pestle ($5\frac{1}{2}$ in or 14·2 cm across) that were used at Jarmo for pounding plants. Opposite a woman of Jericho is shown using a different method, grinding grain in a hollowed-out stone called a quern.

the company of human beings. It only needed one or two more lambs to be found, and a domestic flock was beginning.

On the other hand some hunters, helped by their hunting dogs, may have found that a bigger and steadier supply of food could be obtained by following a flock of wild sheep and occasionally killing one or two animals, rather than by butchering as many animals as possible and then dispersing the remainder.

Once the hunters realized the advantages of farming, they had to learn how to tend their animals and take care of their fields. Some of the ears of wheat found by archaeologists in their villages were mixed up with reed seeds probably picked up accidentally, which suggests that fields were located near swamps, where the damp soil would have produced healthy crops.

A party, doubtless of the younger men, took the flocks and herds to graze on the fine grass which grew on the higher mountain slopes during the summer months. We know this because archaeologists have found the remains of their seasonal camps. The shepherds took shelter with their flocks in large caves when travelling up to the mountain pastures in spring, and again when returning in autumn.

The early farmers did not cease hunting and gathering altogether. Animal bones and charred seeds discovered by archaeologists tell us that gazelles and wild cattle were still tracked down, water birds were trapped, fish were netted in lakes and rivers, and grasses and roots were still collected.

Farming and animal herding meant that food was available at all seasons. Instead of moving to areas where wild plants were ripe or wild animals available, the farmers were able to occupy permanent villages, develop arts and crafts, and live together in far larger social groups than those of their hunting ancestors. Houses had to be built to last. The early farmers lived in mud brick homes, with as many as fifty to a hundred people in each village. New implements had to be made; hoes to help prepare the soil, pestles and mortars for pounding grain, and sickles for the harvest. Those inventive hunters had approached the threshold of a completely new way of life.

3. Life in one of the first towns in the world

The discovery of Catal Huyuk

While hunters and gatherers may have to search for their food over a very wide area, farmers can, if they plan carefully, grow enough food for everybody throughout the year on the land near their village. However, as the population increases some people will have to set out in search of fresh land to till.

The Konya Plain in Turkey is just the sort of area which would have attracted pioneer farmers. The soils are fertile, and its grasslands would have provided abundant food for domestic animals. Some years ago therefore, three archaeologists set out to discover when farmers first occupied the plain. As dusk was approaching on a cold November evening in 1958, they saw in the distance the outline of a low flat-topped mound. Experience at once told them that this might be what they were seeking – the remains of an ancient town. The name of that town is now world famous; it is known as Catal Huyuk.

One of the three, James Mellaart, has since led a team of archaeologists to dig carefully through the many layers of ruined houses which make up the mound of Catal Huyuk. As a result of his excavations, we now know a great deal about life in one of the world's oldest towns.

No one is exactly sure when Catal Huyuk was founded, because the mound is so high that the earliest houses have not yet been uncovered. We know that the city was occupied from 8500 to 7700 years ago, but the first houses may have been built much earlier still. Until those earliest houses at Catal Huyuk are excavated, we shall not know whether the site was first occupied by hunters, who gradually developed farming locally, or by farmers who settled the plain from elsewhere. Certainly, the wild cattle and deer which were to be found on the plain 8500 years ago made it an ideal place for the hunters.

When the Pilgrim Fathers landed in America, one of their first tasks was the planting of their seed corn for the following year's harvest. We can imagine that a similar problem faced the men and women who first lived at Catal Huyuk. Game there was in plenty, but hunting in winter, when the animals drew off to the shelter of the hills, and a carpet of snow stretched into the horizon, was not always successful, and starvation was always a possibility.

The excavations at Catal Huyuk have led to many interesting discoveries about the people who once lived there. We know that new houses were laid out according to an orderly plan, around small courtyards. The builders obtained pieces of timber to shape into logs for house frames. Mud and reeds were mixed and formed into bricks before being laid out in the sun to dry. The men then mortared the bricks together between the timber frames. Houses had flat roofs, and the inside walls were decorated with lively paintings.

The mound of Catal Huyuk can be seen in the distance. Huyuk is Turkish for mound. (The name is pronounced Chat-arl Hoo-yuk.)

One of the pictures which has been uncovered by archaeologists at Catal Huyuk. It shows the town as it appeared to the artist who lived there over 7000 years ago. Notice the clusters of little rectangular houses, and the volcano of Hasan Dag erupting in the far distance.

The people who lived at Catal Huyuk entered their homes by ladder from a hole in the roof, and moved from room to room through little square portholes like the one on the left. We know that they slept on raised platforms, and that their houses each had a main room with an oven in it for baking bread. Their floors were covered with mats. After dark, an oil-burning lamp set in the wall must have sent a warm glow through the rooms.

The inhabitants of Catal Huyuk were able to provide for their basic needs. Spring saw the sowing and lambing, and in autumn the grain bins were filled. Men would go out over the plain with their hunting dogs, to track down the deer, or wild cattle. Hunting not only meant welcome extra meat and skins, but also provided sport and the thrill of danger. Gifts were offered to the goddess of the two leopards on special feast days, marked when the sun rose over a particular mountain peak. Babies were born, and young men grew to adulthood. The old died, and their passing away brought sorrow and mourning. Their bodies were kept in a place apart until their flesh had putrefied. When spring came again, and the rooms were re-plastered to keep out the damp, the corpses were laid in their

A reconstruction of a shrine from Catal Huyuk. Notice the moulded bulls' heads on the far wall and the enormous bulls' horns on the altar.

Religion and art

Special buildings set aside for worship were among the many discoveries made at Catal Huyuk. They were built in the same way as the houses, but their walls were carefully decorated with paintings, models and statues which tell of the life and beliefs of the inhabitants.

The animals of the plain played an important part in religious life. Some shrine walls were decorated with hunting scenes such as the one on the next page in which men clad in caps and kilts of leopard skin are seen loosing arrows at a fleeing deer, while hunting dogs snap and snarl round its heels. In some shrines, models of animals' heads were set into the walls, while in others, benches supporting rows of bulls' horns were built. Another common feature of the shrines is the goddess of the two leopards.

final resting place, under the platforms on which they had slept in life.

With the passing of time, old houses were pulled down to make way for new. Other new homes were built on the outskirts of the town, as the number of people living there steadily grew. Finally, Catal Huyuk covered 33 acres (13 hectares), and the mound rose to be 50 feet (15 metres) above the surrounding plain.

17

below: A woman of Catal Huyuk wore this bracelet of coloured stones and deer teeth, and another used this little (3¾ in or 9·5 cm) bone fork with her make up.

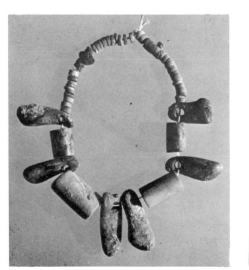

above: A deer hunt drawn by an artist at Catal Huyuk.

Why were these elaborately decorated shrines built? We can only guess on the basis of what was found in them. Many were used for burying the dead, the bones being sprinkled with a red powder, and accompanied by farewell gifts: beautiful mirrors made from obsidian, sharp arrow heads, skilfully carved boxes and necklaces strung with beads of limestone.

Not all corpses were buried in shrines, nor were the shrines used only for burials. One shrine contained gifts of grain, another the bones of wild cattle, and yet another the weapons used for hunting. It appears that the shrines served a number of functions, and we can imagine a select body of priests and priestesses being in charge of their upkeep. Perhaps it was believed that the offering of gifts and prayers to the gods was a necessary part of ensuring enough food in this life, as well as the continuation of life after death.

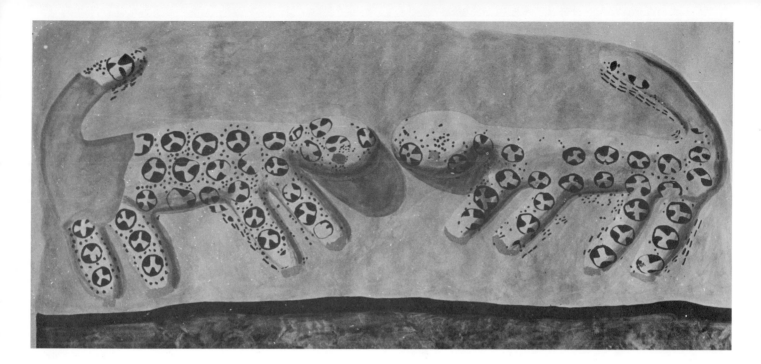

Trade

While the richness of the Konya Plain and the blessing of the gods provided food for all, the raw materials for many of the objects which the archaeologists found at Catal Huyuk must have been obtained by parties going out from the city on prospecting trips, or by trade. Hunters from the hills would see the white rooftops of the town gleaming in the distance and would visit it occasionally with objects for barter. From time to time, well-armed prospecting parties would leave for the source of copper ore in the Taurus Mountains, and would be sure to bring back as well some bags of acorns containing the tannin used to cure leather.

Specialist crafts

Because the farmers at Catal Huyuk were able to grow more food than their families needed, they could have provided food for full-time craftsmen skilled enough to make the delicately painted pottery vessels and wooden caskets which were found there. Objects made from lead and copper also show the

These two leopards were moulded on the wall of a shrine in Catal Huyuk. From the number of layers of plaster it seems that the pictures were renewed about 40 times over the years. Each leopard is nearly 3 ft (92 cm) long.

archaeologist that the people who lived in the town were skilled metal-workers. The importance of this discovery lies in the fact that tools and weapons made of metal are generally more efficient than those of stone. Is it likely that everyone who lived in the town was equally skilled as a painter, a potter, or a metal worker? The answer to this question is surely 'no'. Some people must have been particularly skilled at smelting copper ore, some perhaps spent their time tending the shrines, and others looked after the flocks of sheep. Some of the ovens are so large that they suggest there may even have been full-time bakers.

Within a period of about 4000 years, therefore, some of the people living in the Middle East began to rely more and more upon domestic animals and plants for their food supply. By carefully planning their farming activities, they were able to supply so much food that their settlements grew in size, and they could support specialized craftsmen and priests.

4. Pioneers on the Euphrates plain

While Catal Huyuk developed into a large and prosperous town, people continued to farm among the hills which overlook the valley of the Tigris and Euphrates. On clear days, they could look down on the great plain, stretching far into the horizon. Among the hills, they had winter rains which brought moisture to their fields. They could run their sheep and goats on the nearby grasslands in winter, and take them up to the mountain slopes in the heat of summer.

On the plain however, there was difficulty and danger. Who could control the flood waters which swept over the plain in springtime, only to dry up again in the early summer? How could crops grow when rain was so scarce? Their sheep might die from the heat and lack of water. There was no stone for making arrows or spearheads, nor trees for making homes. For most of the year, the sun beat mercilessly down on a dry, lifeless land.

A view from the great temple at Erech showing the flat Euphrates plain beyond the ruins of the city.

Taming the waters

Like many large rivers, the Euphrates changes its course as it cuts deep into the soft soil of the plain. Over the centuries, it has moved away from its former banks, leaving ridges to show where it once flowed.

Six thousand years ago some of the hill farmers, who had already learned how to divert small mountain streams to water their fields, began to venture onto the plain, and attempted to trap the floodwaters of the Euphrates. Those who succeeded found that they could grow fine crops on soil that was formerly too dry, and graze sheep and cattle on the new pastures.

Their method was, like all great inventions, surprisingly simple. When the spring flood was at its height, water rose above the ridges of the ancient river banks, thus inundating land much higher than the normal river level. During early summer, when the river water began to subside, the bold farmers blocked its exit to the river, thereby forming shallow lakes. This water was then gradually channelled along specially prepared ditches into the fields, its flow being regulated by wooden gates, which shut off the flow when soil in the fields was sufficiently moist. This process is known as irrigation. Today, people in many countries irrigate their land with water trapped behind dams. The discovery was made on the great plain 6000 years ago.

Irrigation brings new riches

In the years that followed the discovery of irrigation, the farmers of the plain were able to grow far more food than they themselves needed. Wheat and barley flourished in the rich fields which surrounded the artificial lakes, and as each of these reservoirs dried out, wild grasses quickly grew, providing grazing for numerous sheep and cattle. The production of so much food was essential because the plain, while rich in soil, was poor in almost everything else. Copper, stone and wood

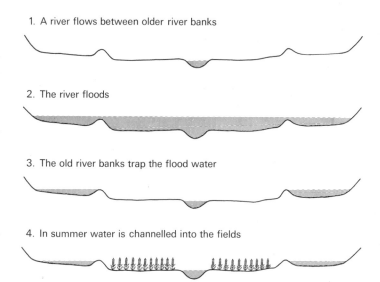

1. A river flows between older river banks

2. The river floods

3. The old river banks trap the flood water

4. In summer water is channelled into the fields

had to be imported from the surrounding hills, and paid for by exporting hides, meat and grain. Enterprising merchants began to use sailing boats on the Euphrates, which they called the 'Urudu.' This word means the 'Copper River' and reminds us that copper ingots were brought down from the north by boat.

Archaeologists who have worked in the Tigris-Euphrates plain have found that the earliest farmers, who are named after the settlement of Ubaid, lived in mud-brick houses which clustered round a temple. The temple played a very important part in village life. Priests gave prayers there for the success of the crops, and supervised the storage of surplus food in its cellars. The priests, too, decided how many sheepskins or bushels of grain should be exchanged for ingots of copper, or planks of timber. Temples then were not only like our churches, but also our banks, with grain and skins taking the place of coins and bills.

The earliest temples of the Ubaid farmers were small, but with time they grew in size and importance. The towns, too,

grew rapidly in size as irrigation provided a secure food supply for a growing population.

Metal tools were probably made for the Ubaid people by wandering smiths, who moved from town to town, mending broken implements and making new tools for sale. The smith was an important person and his visits must have been looked forward to. Copper was particularly valued by Ubaid farmers, because all stone and metal had to be imported. If a stone axe fractured, it had to be thrown away, but if a copper axe broke, it could be melted down and recast. By mending copper tools, therefore, the smith saved farmers the expense of buying new supplies of metal. Although very little is known about the actual way in which the Ubaid metal industry was organized, it is possible that some of the metal tools found by archaeologists were made by smiths who moved from town to town. Let us imagine how an Ubaid town looked as a smith paid one of his visits.

A smith visits an Ubaid town

The smith travels by boat along the maze of interconnecting waterways which now link Ubaid towns. His first glimpse of a settlement as he cranes his neck over the belt of waving reeds is the temple itself. Mounted on a lofty platform over 25 yards (23m) long, the plain forbidding walls with their vertical buttresses dominate the surrounding houses. Having moored his boat, the smith is welcomed by one of the priests' messengers, who has come to escort him to the village.

It is a hot summer day, and the track leads through broad grain fields. Water flows along the nearby irrigation channel. The barley looks healthy: there are few weeds in sight. A party of young children runs to the smith's side, eyeing the strange-looking bellows, moulds and copper ingots which stick out of his leather bag.

Now he enters the town. The houses are made of mud bricks, and through the open doorways he can see glowing bread ovens, food bowls and rush bedding. Water jars lean against the walls, and a dog is curled up in a corner, too hot to concern himself with the passing stranger. Nearing the temple, the smith's sharp eye distinguishes a priestess entering one of the side chapels. She carries a bowl of grain as an offering to Nannar, the moon god, and looks tall and graceful in her high black wig and flowing robe.

The cool of the temple is a refreshing change from the glare of the fields. The chief priest is hospitable, but direct and matter of fact. Several axes are worn out and must be recast, and a copper spearhead has been fractured and needs attention. Negotiations follow. How much barley will the smith ask in return for these tasks? How long will the smith be staying? Surely, two lambskins are too much to ask for such straightforward repair jobs?

When agreement is reached, the smith is provided with lodgings and an area to work. Early the following morning, he begins to build a furnace and prepare the moulds necessary for the work in hand. He works all day, with hardly a pause for rest. The copper is heated to melting point over the charcoal fire, and then carefully poured into the prepared moulds. A young boy helps the smith by pumping the bellows with his feet. He watches in silent admiration as the smith turns out the bright new axes and the spear from their moulds, and trims them off. The priest is pleased with the work and gives the smith two bags of barley, a sack containing dried meat, and a lambskin, with the instructions that they be carried to his boat. Before long, the smith is once again on his way, heading along the canals and rivers to the next town on his round.

5. Town to city

The Ubaid people are most important to our story, because they learned how to irrigate the rich soils of the plain. At first, their settlements were no more than villages, but the increased population made possible by the prosperity of irrigation farming soon led to the growth of cities.

The trading of food and skins for other raw materials was an important part of the Ubaid way of life. Archaeologists have found some of the trade goods, such as copper and gemstones. We can imagine the merchants arranging trade exchanges, and the river barges arriving with their valuable cargo.

Out of this very prosperity arose a problem. How were the merchants to record their sales? How were the priests, who supervised the temple storerooms, to remember who had deposited their share of grain, and who had not?

The beginning of writing

The answer to the problem was both simple and obvious. Slabs of wet clay were prepared, onto which the merchants recorded their dealings by impressing pictures. These pictures had particular meanings: ⌀ meant a fat-tailed sheep, and ≁ meant water. Other signs were used to denote honey, cattle, meat and fish. You can probably recognize the meaning of some symbols in the picture on the right. Soon signs for numbers and people were devised so that clerks could note, for example, the number of cattle delivered to the temple by a given person. Once the tablet was full, it was allowed to dry, thus providing a permanent record of trading agreements. Many of the clay tablets have survived to this day, and tell us of exchanges made 5500 years ago.

Archaeologists distinguish the people who learned the use of writing from the illiterate Ubaid farmers by the name 'Uruk.' Uruk itself (or Erech as it came to be called) was one of their largest settlements.

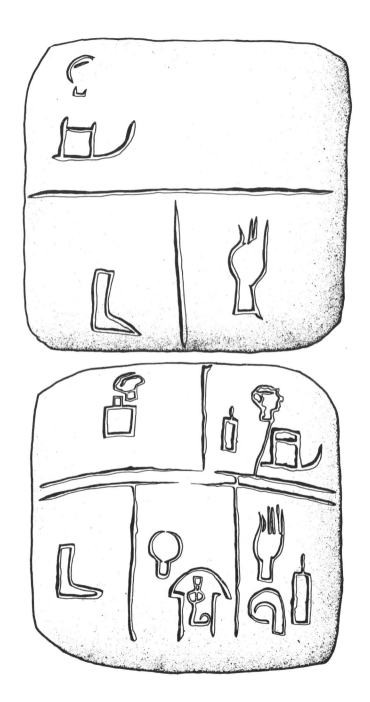

Two sides of a tablet from the Sumerian city of Kish, showing early writing. The tablet is about 5500 years old.

Towns grow into cities

The trade goods which flowed into the cities of the plain led to a new, more vigorous and exciting way of life for their inhabitants. Indeed, the smith who a hundred years earlier had travelled between Ubaid towns would hardly have recognized the bustle and activity of the new cities. He would also have found little work in the city, unless he joined a team of smiths permanently employed by the temple authorities.

Some of the differences between Ubaid towns and Uruk cities were a matter of scale, rather like the differences between a small country town and a major port today. Uruk temples were much larger, and were more lavishly decorated. Imported limestone slabs provided solid foundations. Inside the temple itself were huge columns 2 yards (1·8m) wide at the base, which supported lofty ceilings decorated with flowers modelled from clay. Many priests now ran the temple affairs where there had once been only one or two. Rooms were set aside for storing the grain, dates, sheepskins and dried fish which farmers and fishermen paid as taxes. Much land was now owned by the temple itself and the labourers had to be housed and fed by the authorities.

The survival of Uruk writing tablets allows us to find out more about the Uruk people than we know about their Ubaid ancestors. We know from the Erech temple records that there were special classes of craftsmen. The Uruk word for a carpenter was *Naggar*, a word still used in modern Arabic and having just the same meaning. Special words for the chief smith, chief herdsman, and chief priest were also in use. There were groups of artists, who decorated all kinds of objects with religious themes and scenes from everyday life. Here, for example, a priest is seen offering a bowl of fruit to the goddess Inanna, who stands dressed in a long kilt and hat. There are other examples on the next pages.

From the temple records, we know that there was a flourishing trade in human beings, for slave girls were brought from the Persian hills to serve foreign masters. We can see, therefore, that from the high priests to merchants, clerks and farm labourers, and so down to the humblest slave girl, the Uruk cities sheltered many classes of people.

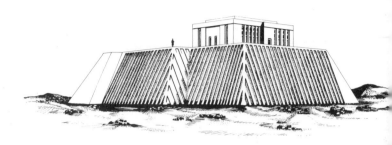

The White Temple at Erech as it would have looked 5000 years ago.

A detail of the carving on the alabaster vase shown on page 26.

25

Each had its different duties and tasks. Merchants had already used sailing boats on the Euphrates during Ubaid times. Now, they also used wheeled waggons. No one is sure where the wheel was invented but the earliest known picture of a wheeled vehicle has been found on a clay tablet from the city of Erech itself. These 'covered waggons' would have greatly increased trade. Oxen were used to haul grain waggons from the fields to the temple store rooms. There, the amount of grain was recorded and the sacks stored until needed.

The potter also used the wheel for shaping clay vessels. Many tall drinking cups with elegant spouts, cups with high handles, and simple eating bowls were made to satisfy the demands of a large city population.

The Uruk people, who lived on the Euphrates plain between 5500 and 5000 years ago, were very inventive. Archaeologists regard them as the originators of a civilized life in the Euphrates valley. They lived in the world's first cities, invented writing, developed the wheel for speeding transport, and built monumental temples for worship and city administration.

They did not suddenly disappear from history, 5000 years ago. Archaeologists simply use the word 'Uruk' to describe the period when those discoveries were made. Their descendants are called the Sumerians. It was with the Sumerians that the ancient civilization of the plain reached its zenith.

A clay tablet found at Erech is the earliest evidence for wheeled vehicles.
This is the way they are shown.

An alabaster vase from Erech, height 3 ft (92 cm), showing the produce of crops and herds being carried in procession and offered to the goddess Inanna.

An early Sumerian stone carving shows bronze smiths at work. The chief smith, dressed in a long kilt seems to be supervising three apprentices.

left: A stone carving from Ubaid of a Sumerian official whose name was probably Kur-lil. Height 15 in (37.5 cm).

right: A Sumerian couple drawn from the original carvings found at Tell Asmar. Although they were probably meant to represent a god and goddess they show well the Sumerian style of dress.

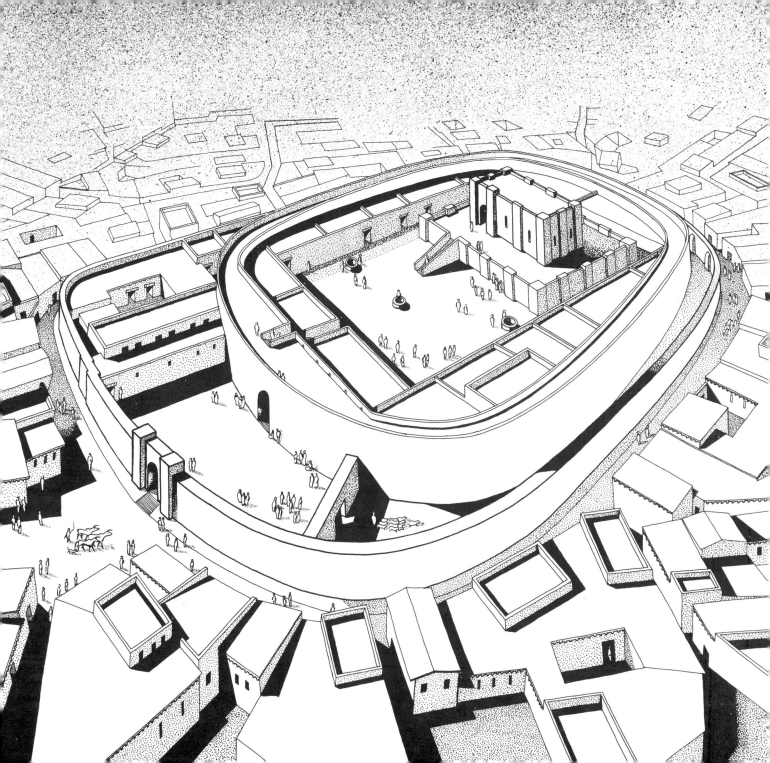

6. The Sumerians

Who were the Sumerians?

When the early written tablets were translated, it was found that the scribes called their land between the Tigris and Euphrates 'Sumer'. Archaeologists have, therefore, called the people who lived there 'Sumerians'. In time, the same region came to be called Babylonia, and today it is called Iraq.

The Sumerians, who were descended directly from the Uruk people, lived from 5000 to 4000 years ago. This chapter is about their achievements.

A bird's-eye view of a Sumerian city

Sumerian cities were each dominated by a lofty temple. Some temples were so large that their ruins dominate the landscape to this day. In this reconstruction of a Sumerian city, the temple is set apart from the surrounding buildings by two sets of high walls. Guards stand at the main gates to prevent unauthorized entry. Offices, store-rooms and shrines are grouped round the temple court, which provides a dignified contrast to the sprawling houses which cluster outside the walls. If you look closely you can see a herd of sheep being driven into the temple. They are doubtless part of a farmer's annual tax. The city itself is also surrounded by walls, because disputes between cities over land ownership or water rights are sometimes settled by war.

A distant part of the city has been assigned to foreign merchants. Their quarters are comfortable, for they may stay several weeks before returning to their own cities.

The Sumerian cities are much larger than those of the Uruk period. The city of Erech covers 1100 acres (440 hectares), and has a population of about 24,000 people. Sumerians are proud of their cities, whose gleaming white walls offer refuge in times of danger, and whose markets provide trading opportunities.

A bird's-eye view of Khafajah, a Sumerian city.

The interior of Mes-kalam-du's coffin. Notice the gold helmet and bowls.

A Sumerian cemetery

Cemeteries provide the archaeologist with much information. In 1922, Sir Leonard Woolley discovered a Sumerian cemetery at the city of Ur. Over 2000 graves were uncovered. The bodies had been placed in plain coffins of wood or clay. They were accompanied by a few personal possessions, such as daggers, and had decorative pins to fasten the shroud. Cups containing food and drink were placed in the grave, and covered with reed matting, to protect them from the damp soil. The graves contained the bodies of the men and women who lived at Ur about 5000 years ago.

A few graves, however, stood out because of the precious offerings buried with the dead. Two golden bowls from one such grave describe their owner as 'Mes-kalam-du, Hero of the Good Land'. He was buried wearing a magnificent helmet

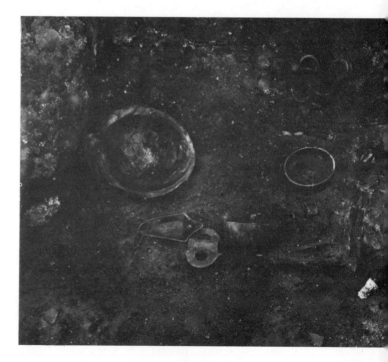

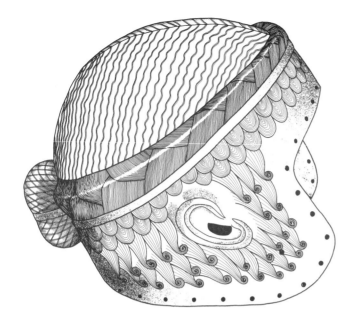

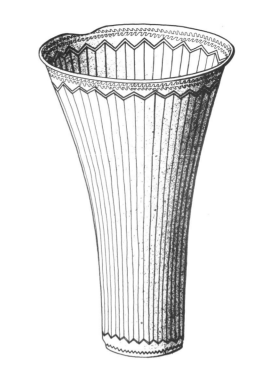

The helmet of Prince Mes-kalam-du.
The engraving imitates the prince's hair and shows it
tied in a 'bun' at the back.

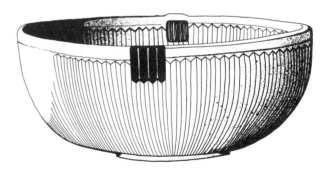

A flask and bowl of gold from graves in the cemetery
of Ur.

of gold and silver. His spears and daggers had golden handles,
and the food and drink to sustain him in the after life were
stored in vessels of silver and gold.

Mes-kalam-du was clearly a more important person than
the people buried in the simpler graves. He may have been a
royal prince, who had been given honours and riches as a result of success in battle.

Already, Sir Leonard Woolley had discovered the grave of a
Sumerian hero. In 1928, he was to find the tombs of A-bar-gi
and Pu-abi, the king and queen of the city of Ur.

The tomb of King A-bar-gi

The first hint that he was on the verge of an exciting discovery
came when five skeletons were found, lying side by side, on a

downward-sloping ramp. Each skeleton lay on reed matting beside a copper dagger and a small pottery cup. The ramp led down to a broad chamber, which revealed one of the most amazing sights ever seen by an archaeologist. Its floor was covered with skeletons. Here, laid out in neat rows, were the remains of ten court ladies, each wearing a diadem of gold and precious stones. The body of a lyre player had been laid beyond them. She wore a golden crown, and her lyre was decorated with a bull's head, fashioned in gold and lapis lazuli. There, were the bodies of grooms stretched out beside the oxen, which had dutifully drawn the royal carriage to its final resting place. Ranks of soldiers had died in that vault. Their skeletons lay in military order. Helmets still protected their skulls, and copper spears lay by their sides. Nine ladies-in-waiting accompanied their dead master, dressed, as befitted the occasion, in all their finery: gold earings, head-dresses of gold, carnelian and lapis lazuli, and golden necklaces.

Many of the king's servants were buried with their royal master. The picture on the next page shows the scene as the grooms and ladies in waiting were about to drink poison and prepare for death. Afterwards, priests entered the hall, arranged the bodies in an orderly fashion, placed the lyre over the dead musician, and killed the oxen. Five thousand years were to elapse before the light of day again entered the burial chamber.

This was the retinue of King A-bar-gi. Sumerian robbers had looted the grave during the construction of his queen's tomb nearby, so we know nothing of his own finery. Queen Pu-abi's tomb, however, was found intact. Laid out on a wooden bier, the queen wore a large wig, surmounted by a crown of beech and willow leaves finely made from pure gold. In this picture, you can see how she may have looked. She was buried wearing a cape made up of beads of gold, silver, agate and lapis lazuli. The pictures on page 33 show some of the objects found in her tomb.

The cemetery at Ur tells us that the Sumerian community was made up of many different groups of people. Some were important, and wielded much authority. Kings made great decisions of state, and were responsible for the defence and administration of the city. They were immensely rich, and employed many servants. Stone masons, farmers and merchants were also buried in the cemetery at Ur. Their toil and annual taxes provided the city with wealth, and its ruler with power.

A board used for a game that must have been something like checkers. It is decorated with lapis-lazuli, red limestone and shell. Two sets of counter pieces such as were used with this game are also shown. The board is 11¾ in.(29.8 cm) long.

right: A silver flask 7½ in (19 cm) high. Flasks like this were used to carry offerings to the gods.

far right: A necklace and bracelet made of gold and lapis lazuli. The necklace is 8½ in (21 cm long).

Sumerian farming

The thriving cities were dependent on the irrigation of the rich soils of the plain. Sumerian farmers, using ox-drawn plows, brought much new land into production. Sometimes the Sumerians made decorative scenes of farming activities like the one below. They also kept written records of the farmers' tasks.

One of the Sumerian writing tablets gives a farmer's advice to his son. This document allows us to see how careful the farmers were to ensure a good harvest.

The farmer's round began in May, when he opened up the sluice gates to flood the field. When the waters had subsided, he fenced the field to keep oxen or irresponsible people from tramping over the soggy soil. Imagine how difficult plowing would have been if the field was broken up by ruts and bumps.

When the topsoil was sufficiently firm, all weeds and stubble were cleared, and the soil was broken up at least twice before being hoed. The farmer was anxious to break up big clods of earth, because barley grows best if the soil is thoroughly aerated.

Then came one of the most important parts of the yearly round. The farmer hitched two oxen to the plow, prepared the bags of seed barley, and began plowing and sowing in one action. There was a funnel in the plow to direct the barley straight down into the furrow. Small boys ran behind the plow removing clods of earth from the furrow, for nothing must hinder the barley once it began to sprout.

When the first shoots appeared, the farmer prayed to Ninkilim, the goddess of mice, to see that vermin did not ruin the crop. Birds, too, were scared off the growing barley. The diligent farmer saw that the crops were watered regularly during the growing season or the yield of grain would hardly have justified all his earlier work.

Timing the harvest was a task for the expert. It had to begin before the plants began to bend under their own weight. Teams of three men then went out to cut, collect and transport the barley to the threshing floor, where it was winnowed and bagged up. Only then could the good farmer relax his vigilance.

A Sumerian dairy. A cow is being milked while its calf stands near. On the left, the milk is being poured into large jars. From a temple frieze at Ubaid made with limestone figures on a bituminous stone background $8\frac{3}{4}$ in (22 cm) high.

Irrigation

One difficult problem faced by Sumerian farmers was that the level of the Euphrates rose quickly, and at the wrong time of the year for crops. Just as plowing was complete, the fields were likely to be flooded. Then during summer, when the river was at its lowest, the crops were most in need of water. So the Sumerians controlled the floods by building an elaborate network of canals, dams and reservoirs. Instead of devastating the fields, water was stored in reservoirs, and let out during the summer months. By constructing new canals and reservoirs, the Sumerians brought much new land into use to feed the growing city population. The city authorities not only organized the labour necessary to dig canals and reservoirs, but also kept the irrigation works in good repair. Canals could gradually silt up, and sometimes flood water destroyed the dams. It is hardly surprising, therefore, to find that a special force of inspectors, known as the *gagullu,* was established. They constantly patrolled the canal system, on the lookout for signs of disrepair. Part of their task was to stop illegal poaching of water, and to maintain law and order.

A clay tablet showing a map of the fields and canals near Nippur is shown below left. On the right is a key giving a translation of the names on the map.

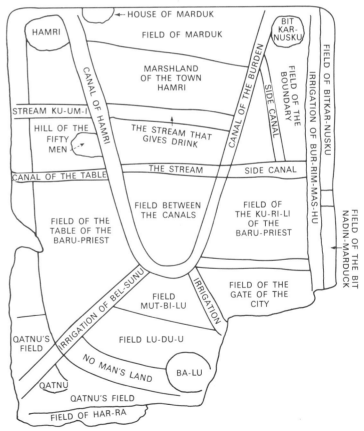

Sumerian schooldays

Some farmers owned their own land, but others were employed by wealthy nobles, who held posts at court or in the temple. The sons of noblemen or successful merchants were sent to school, where their education was designed to ensure them a successful career. Archaeologists have occasionally discovered Sumerian school 'exercise books.' Some such tablets contain the same sentence carefully copied out a number of times. In others, we can read the schoolmaster's corrections. One pupil had obviously been very dull. His teacher had put a line straight through his careless work.

Schooldays were long, and the work difficult. Pupils arrived at sunrise, and left at sunset. They were beaten if they did not work hard, or behaved badly. Each school had a headmaster, form masters, and teachers who specialized in mathematics, literature and grammar.

One well known Sumerian story recalls a boy's first day at school. He prepared his clay tablet, and was given an exercise to copy. After his lunch, he attended a recitation class, followed by more written work. That evening, he went to bed early, because he was anxious not to arrive late the next day. He was up at first light, and urged his mother to prepare his lunch as fast as possible. Let the schoolboy take up his own story.

'When I awoke early in the morning, I faced my mother and said to her: Give me my lunch, I want to go to school. My mother gave me two rolls and I went to school.'

But the schoolboy's luck was bad that day. He was beaten for careless work, for talking, for standing up out of turn, and for walking out of the school gate before sunset.

During his second year at school, the same boy grew conceited with his own ability. Things became so bad that he refused to obey his masters' instructions, and there was a brawl in the class room. Finally, the headmaster heard the noise of the fighting, and warned the boy that if he did not behave in future, he would be severely punished.

Other boys were better behaved, and grew up to play an important part in the life of their community. Some became surveyors, and accurately sub-divided new agricultural land, or designed the path of irrigation canals. Others, with their knowledge of mathematics, designed temples and palaces, or kept the temple accounts in order.

The Sumerian schoolmaster thought this work unsatisfactory.

Housing and furniture

Most Sumerian houses were made of mud-bricks. The thick walls and small windows kept the room cool in summer and warm in winter. Some rooms had built-in benches, but wooden beds, tables and chairs were also used. Wooden grilles covered the windows, and doors were so low that it was necessary to stoop when going from one room to another. At night a light was obtained from lamps burning oil from the seed of the sesame plant.

No carpets, curtains, blankets or sheets have survived, and archaeologists are not sure whether or not they were used. Bracelets, earrings, lipstick and mirrors have been found in typical Sumerian houses.

Homes of the wealthy were large and well furnished. Some even contained bathrooms, and lavatories built over drains which connected with the rivers. City streets were no more than winding, ill-lit alleyways, whose layout resulted more from accident than design. When a house was in danger of collapse, it was levelled to make way for a new building. There was no set plan for a new home, rooms being built to suit the shape of the available site. House collapse was such a constant worry that laws were made ruling that if a wall fell and killed anyone, the builder responsible would be put to death.

We would consider that most Sumerian houses were dark, unhygienic hovels. We would be alarmed by the snakes which lingered in the thatch searching out rats and mice. But the people who lived in them may have been glad of the shelter of city life, reassured that the food stored in the temple vaults was available if the harvest failed.

A model of a Sumerian house made of baked clay found at Mari on the Euphrates. Diameter 21$\frac{1}{4}$ in (54 cm).

The cylinder seal and metalwork

When a Sumerian wished to mark his own property, or add his name to a contract, he used his own particular seal. These seals were made of a semi-precious stone, and shaped like cylinders. A scene of daily or religious life was carved on the surface of the cylinder, so that its impression could be rolled onto the surface of soft clay.

Many seals were expertly made, and the scenes they portray tell us much about the Sumerians themselves. Here, for example, we see two goddesses bringing a worshipper to a seated god. Notice the god's elegant chair, and the flowing robes of the goddess. This intricate picture is contained on a seal no more than an inch high.

Expert craftsmen were employed to make seals. Their ability was appreciated by priest and king alike. We have seen how Queen Pu-abi and her court wore skilfully made ornaments of gold, silver and precious stone. The jeweller's mastery of gold and silver was matched by the skill with which the smith made metal tools.

below left: A scene carved in relief around a 4000-year-old Sumerian cylinder seal. Goddesses and worshipper approach the god with raised hands. On the right is Sumerian writing.

below: One of the cylinder seals found in the grave of Queen Pu-abi shows a man and a woman sitting drinking while servants wait on them. A similar scene is shown on the lower half of the seal. The cylinder is nearly 2 in (4·9 cm) high with a diameter of about 1 in (2·3 cm).

Sumerian smiths knew that by mixing copper and tin to make bronze, they could cast tools harder and of a more intricate design than was possible with copper alone. Farmers used bronze sickles. Improved types of axe, chisel and adze were designed, making the carpenter's work quicker and easier. Long tubes were made to serve the same function as our drinking straws. Ear-picks, tweezers and mirrors were manufactured for the luxury market, while bronze cauldrons on wheels were made for service in the temple.

The royal workshops hummed with activity, for the security of the city depended on the steady flow of weapons and armour. The king who employed most smiths was inevitably a ruler of great influence.

A Sumerian drinking through a metal tube.

Kings

In times of danger, Sumerians elected a lugal to lead them. Lugal meant 'great man' or 'great householder'. He may have had no connection with the temple, and after the crisis was over, he became a normal citizen again. Some leaders, however, having tasted power, were reluctant to give it up. They stayed on at the head of their army, and set themselves up as permanent kings.

The kings had many important duties to fulfil. Some were to do with the administration of the city, others were concerned with its defence.

Some kings regarded it as their duty to protect the helpless. On one occasion, a royal messenger died, leaving an orphan son without protection. The matter was brought to the attention of the king, who saw that the child was cared for. Usually, orphans were looked after by aunts and uncles, or couples with no children of their own.

The king was also responsible for justice. Laws were essential in a thriving city. The earliest laws we know about were laid down by King Ur-nammu. One of his laws stated: 'If a man has broken another man's bones with a weapon, he will pay one mina of silver.' A law of King Lipit-ishtar stated: 'If a man has hired an ox and damaged its eye, he shall pay half of its value to the owner.'

These laws are important, because they show us clearly that city life was made as orderly and fair as possible. Anyone who felt himself cheated could turn to the law for protection. Consider how important laws are for us. They were just as important for the Sumerians.

The king of each city was wealthy, and commanded many soldiers. Armies were equipped with chariots, and the soldiers were armed with metal spears and daggers. Some of the kings did not look for power beyond the walls of their own cities. Others were more ambitious, and dreamed of conquest. We know the names of the warlike kings. Lugalzagesi of Umma ruled Sumer from his capital at Erech. The mighty Sargon of Agade succeeded to the throne of all Sumer in 2370 BC.

Sargon's power stretched even beyond the borders of Sumer. At first, he tightened his grip on Sumerian cities by destroying their walls, taking hostages, and installing his own picked followers as governors. Then he began wars of conquest. On one campaign 600 miles (960 km) to the north of Ur, he saved a colony of Sumerian merchants from the attacks of the local king.

His empire was further enlarged by Naram-Sin, his grandson, who defeated the warlike hill-tribes whose presence threatened the cities in the plain. A picture of Naram-Sin at the head of his victorious troops is still in existence. He went on to build fortresses at Brak and Nineveh, to protect the civilized Sumerians from surprise attack. Trade flourished under the protection of so powerful a king. A priest of the time could boast that captive apes and mighty elephants from distant lands abounded in the great square of the capital, a claim which suggests that Naram-Sin's merchants had reached even into India.

Under the rule of Naram-Sin's son Sharkalisharri, the Sumerians were defeated by an alliance of hill-tribes known as the Gutians. These warriors swept down on the populous cities, destroying and pillaging as they went. In later times the Gutians were remembered with awe. They were barbarians, unaccustomed to the benefits of civilized life.

The Gutians did not destroy all the cities of Sumer, for a century after their appearance Utu-Hengal, the ruler of Erech,

defeated the last Gutian chief. A flowering of civilized city life followed. As in the time of Naram-Sin, one king held sway over an empire which stretched beyond the borders of Sumer. But the hill-dwellers were to come back again. This time, there was to be no revival. Four thousand years ago, the Sumerians passed from history. When civilization came again to the land between the two rivers, the country was to be known as Babylonia.

below left: A bronze portrait of King Sargon (nearly lifesize).

This sandstone pillar commemorates a victory of Naram-Sin, king of Agade. One of the enemy has a broken spear. The pillar is 6 ft 6½ in (2 m) high.

7. The Sumerians in war and peace

Excavations of Sumerian cities have produced much evidence for the way of life of the people who once lived in them. Numerous clay writing tablets tell us of the clerks who saw that the king's commands were acted upon. We can read of the trading missions which took Sumerian ships to Dilmun for supplies of copper. A beautiful shell and lapis lazuli box from Ur is decorated with scenes of the Sumerian army at war, and the celebrations which followed victory. This type of evidence provides the archaeologist with a clear picture of trade, bronze working and Sumerian warfare.

We can imagine that a royal campaign against desert nomads may well have begun with a clerk in one of the temple offices preparing a tablet of wet clay and writing instructions for a trading mission to Dilmun. New supplies of copper are necessary in order to equip a military expedition.

He picks up his reed stylus and inscribes his orders.

'To the keeper of the royal warehouse. Please prepare 15 barrels of sesame oil, 100 lengths of fine woollen cloth, and 80 sacks of first grade barley. Seal all containers with the stamp of the controller-general of the royal household, and send me a signed receipt from the captain of the *Arrow*. Have the goods transported to pier 3 one week hence.'

signed, Nin-dada, royal scribe

'To the captain of the ship *Arrow*. On behalf of the king, I order you to proceed eight days hence to Dilmun. You are to take 15 barrels of sesame oil, 100 lengths of fine woollen cloth, 80 sacks of barley. You are to exchange these, as the market permits, for not less than 150 copper ingots, 50 sections of ivory and 50 planks of cedarwood. You will be issued with the usual pass, and your vessel will be supplied in the normal way. Payment will be made on successful completion.'

signed, Nin-dada, royal scribe

A messenger takes the tablets to the warehouse, where a keeper files the instructions, and arranges for 12 waggons to be booked for the following week. Then the messenger hurries to the wharf to look for the skipper of the merchant ship *Arrow*.

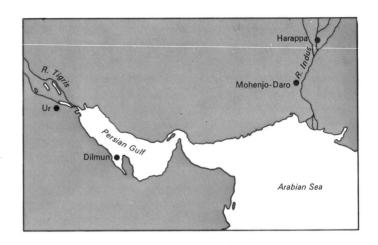

A voyage to Dilmun

On the appointed day, a convoy of ox-driven carts slowly makes its way to the pier. The port is alive with activity. Burly sailors begin loading cargo into the hold. A clerk checks each item against his list before asking the captain for his receipt. Part of the clay is moistened, the captain rolls his personal cylinder seal across it, and prepares to leave port.

By early afternoon, the skyline of Ur is dipping over the horizon. At first, *Arrow* passes a few small fishing boats, but she is soon alone in the open sea. For four days and five nights she heads southwards.

On the morning of the fifth day, land is sighted on the starboard bow. Other ships are now visible, for *Arrow* is only a couple of hours sailing from Dilmun. Some ships are from Sumer, but others are of an unfamiliar type. The captain points out the differences to a new member of his crew. That one comes from Egypt, and those come from the great cities of the Indus Valley in the distant east.

Now *Arrow* heaves-to outside port. Her cargo has to be inspected by the Dilmun authorities before she can proceed. Lo-

cal officials check the ship's hold, and calculate the taxes due to the ruler of Dilmun, before issuing a permit to trade. By evening, the ship is berthed, and the crew members are allowed to go ashore.

A Sumerian's first visit to Dilmun is never forgotten. From childhood, he has regarded Sumer as the very centre of the world, and certainly the only country to lay claim to being civilized. Yet here at Dilmun, a few days sailing from Sumer, he sees city walls as great as those at Ur, and the comfortable houses of local merchants. He meets merchants from the cities of other civilized countries. Egyptians from Abydos and Thebes bring copper and precious stones mined in the Sinai desert. The cities of the Indus Valley are also represented. Their traders claim that their cities of Mohenjo-Daro and Harappa are larger and richer than Ur itself. Certainly, the benefits of irrigation are not confined to Sumer, for the waters of the Nile and the Indus have also been turned to the benefit of man. Other people have developed civilization. They too have a system of writing, and a strong method of government.

When the transactions have been completed, the ship returns to Ur, with its cargo of copper, timber and ivory.

Not much is known about the kind of boats the Sumerians used. Archaeologists can get some idea from the models found in graves and from drawings on cylinder seals. The seal impression above (1½ in. or 3.6 cm high) shows a high-prowed boat. A long-haired figure pushes the boat with a pole, while another sits in the boat. The model below is 29 in. (75 cm) long. These models were loaded with a cargo of pottery or copper vessels possibly representing food for the dead.

The bronze foundry

Back in Ur, the preparations for war continue. The chief smith Ubar-sin arrives at work to find an order for 300 new spearheads awaiting him. He sets to work calculating the amount of copper, tin and wood he will need, and instructs his foreman to prepare clay moulds in which to cast the spears. By mid-morning he is on his way to the warehouse with the order, and a requisition for the necessary materials. Some of the ingots brought back by the *Arrow* are assigned to his workshop, and their delivery is arranged.

The wood for his furnace has been carried by barge down the Euphrates. It is still green, because dry, well-seasoned wood does not make good charcoal.

Now the chief smith and his assistant can turn to the task in hand. Each stage in the casting process must be perfectly performed. The clay moulds are ready. Each has two distinct halves, into which the shape of a spearhead has been cut. The two halves are clamped together, and tightly bound round with metal bands.

A couple of apprentices are cutting up the wood and stacking it next to the furnace. Another has brought out the bellows, and now attaches them to a nozzle. A constant draft is essential if the charcoal is to become hot enough to melt copper. There are no written instructions for the young apprentices. Their trade is learned by experience. Each master smith has his own little secrets and is reluctant to part with them.

As soon as the fire has been fanned to a deep, fiery glow, the chief smith brings a crucible containing chunks of copper, and places it among the charcoal. The bellows are constantly pumped, and beads of molten metal begin to drop to the bottom of the crucible. When all the copper has melted, the smith drops in some small pellets of tin, and occasionally stirs the mixture as only he knows how.

When the moulds are set in line and the metal binding strips wedged into position, the chief grasps his tongs and carefully lifts the red-hot crucible. Gingerly he walks to the moulds, and pours the hissing liquid into their hollow centres. Soon after, when the metal has cooled and set, an apprentice removes the wedges holding the bands in place and pries the two halves of the moulds apart. The master craftsman inspects the new bronze spearhead critically. It must be carefully finished. All casting marks must be removed before the tip and cutting edges are hammered to give them extra strength. Then the routine of the previous day continues. When the weapons are complete, they are delivered to the royal arsenal, and the campaign can begin.

A Sumerian king Eannatum of Lagash leads his troops into battle. Notice the soldiers' spears, shields and helmets and the Sumerian writing in the background. From a stone carving found at Tello.

A victorious battle

A series of forced marches brings the army to the area where some Sumerian merchants have been attacked by desert brigands. They are joined there by the king and his military advisers, who have come up by boat. Scouts have already located the offending tribesmen. Their camp is sited three hours' march to the west. They confirm that it is on level ground, suitable for a chariot attack.

A cloud of dust rises as the well-disciplined Sumerian army moves forward to attack the enemy. Will the enemy see and scatter into the desert? The answer soon comes. Imagining that another merchant caravan is within their grasp, they arrogantly approach the Sumerian army. The chariot horses break first into a trot, then a gallop. What a wonderful sight, as the chariots in battle order close with the enemy. Spearmen are poised. The echoing orders of an officer drift back across the dusty plain, and already the first desert dwellers fall before the withering volley of spears. The chariots wheel around with one accord, and smash once more against the disorganized enemy.

Drums sound. The infantry moves forward in close order.

They are to deal the death blow. Caught between chariots and the advancing infantry, the desert dwellers are trapped. Some surrender, others lie dead. Yet others are mortally wounded, and an officer finishes them off with a sword.

What of the captives? The king has alighted from his chariot and watches as they are paraded before him. A net is cast over them and they are left out in the burning sun. Soon they will be taken into slavery.

A feast is held that same evening to celebrate victory, and offer thanks to the god of war. Senior officials congratulate the king on his victory. Servants bustle round with food and drink, while a singer and lyre-player perform the king's favourite melodies. The Sumerian traders will be safe in future. The royal barge is then prepared for its triumphant return to Ur.

After the battle, a singer accompanied on a lyre performed for the king and his nobles. A scene from the box mentioned on page 42.

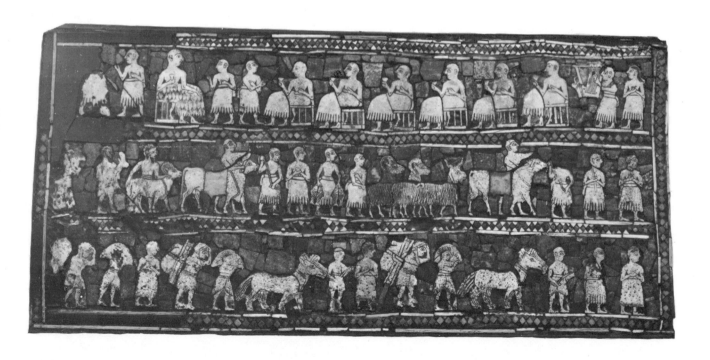

8. What has archaeology shown us?

There was a time when people who wished to find out about the past turned only to ancient writings or to tales handed down by word of mouth. Now, however, archaeologists can find out what happened long before even writing itself was invented, by digging up and studying the remains from prehistoric settlements.

What have archaeologists learned from their excavations? They have found that for an immense period of time, about two million years, people obtained all their food by hunting, gathering and fishing. It was only fairly recently, about 12,000 years ago, that certain groups of hunters in different parts of the world began to learn how to farm.

This was one of prehistoric man's most important discoveries. Farmers can normally produce far more food than can hunters or gatherers. The extra food produced by farmers made it possible for some people to spend their time developing such skills as metal working and writing.

This discovery of farming, therefore, made possible many more discoveries. Some people could now live all the year round in the same place practicing their craft, while others could spend their working hours on distant trading missions. Before long, villages grew into towns, and towns into cities. Farmers discovered better ways of farming, and cities became richer.

Some of these discoveries soon spread, as more people began to realize the benefits of farming and civilization.

In some countries, however, farming is still only a recent development, while in others, bands of hunters and gatherers are found to this day.

The discoveries which archaeologists have made and are still making help us to understand how and when our ancestors made important discoveries and explain the many different ways of life to be found in the world today.

These three pictures show the changing way of life of the first farmers and city dwellers. At the top is a hunters' camp. The hunters gradually developed farming and their homes became increasingly solid and well-built. Finally villages grew into cities with fine temples and storehouses.

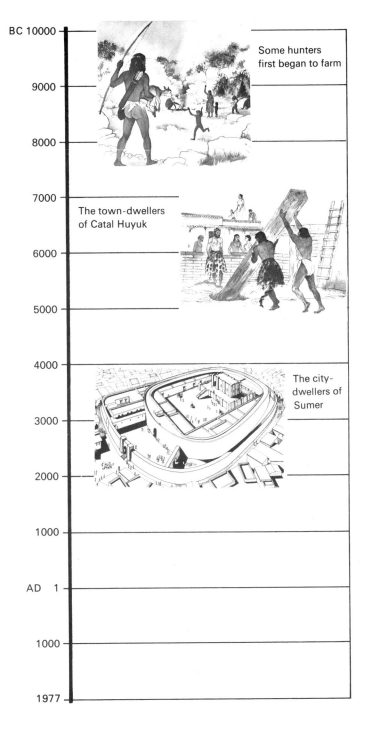

BC 10000
9000
8000
7000
6000
5000
4000
3000
2000
1000
AD 1
1000
1977

Some hunters first began to farm

The town-dwellers of Catal Huyuk

The city-dwellers of Sumer

Index

Acknowledgments

Illustrations in this volume are reproduced by kind permission of the following:

front cover, back cover, pp. 27 (statue), 29,33,39,43 (bitumen boat), 47, Trustees of the British Museum; p. 5. C. Higham; p. 7 after K.P. Oakley *Framework for dating fossil man* (Weidenfeld & Nicholson); p. 7 (wheat) Cambridge University Museum of Archaeology and Anthropology; pp. 10, 12, 43, Oriental Institute, University of Chicago, from Braidwood & Howe *Prehistoric investigations in Iraqi Kurdistan;* p. 8 from Clark & Piggott, *Prehistoric societies* (Hutchinson); pp. 15, 16 17, 18, 19, J. Mellaart; pp. 20, 25 (alabaster vase), 26 (alabaster vase), 35, 38, 41, 45, Hirmer Fotoarchiv Munchen; p. 25 White Temple from the *Dawn of Civilization*, S. Piggott, (Thames & Hudson); pp. 28, 39 (drawing) after M. Mallowan, *Early Mesopotamia and Iran* (Thames & Hudson); pp. 36, 37, The University Museum of the University of Pennsylvania; p. 36 (plan) from Singer & Holmyard, *A history of technology* (OUP).

Drawings by Maurice Wilson and Peter Duncan

Drawings on pp. 11, 13, 14, 22, 32, 34, 44 and 46 are by Maurice Wilson; drawings on pp. 6, 9, 21, 26, 27, 30, 31, 39 and 41 are by Peter Duncan.

cover: Part of the mosaic decoration on the famous 'Royal Standard of Ur'. This box-like object is described on page 42. On the front cover you can see scenes of peace with Sumerian nobles drinking at a victory feast, and servants or prisoners bringing tributes of cattle and sheep for the king. On the back cover the Sumerian king's chariots and pikemen are preparing battle.

The Cambridge History Library

The Cambridge Introduction to History
Written by Trevor Cairns

The Cambridge Topic Books
General Editor Trevor Cairns

Lerner Publications Company
241 First Avenue North, Minneapolis, Minnesota 55401